Samsung Galaxy S24 User manual For Beginners and Seniors

A comprehensive User Guide For Beginners and Seniors to explore the multifaceted capabilities of the Samsung Galaxy S24 Ultra 5G like a pro.

Precious Livestone

Table of Contents

INTRODUCTION..10

Your device set up...11

Chapter One 13

On your device 13

Use the setup wizard..14

Get data from old devices 14

Lock or unlock your device...................................15

Side button settings 15

Click twice..15

Press and hold..16

Account 16

Add google account 16

Add Samsung account...17

Add Outlook account 17

Set up voicemail...18

navigation 18

Press 19

Swipe 19

Drag and drop..20

Zoom in and out 20

Touch and hold..21

Navigation Bar 22

Navigation buttons 23

Navigation gestures 23

Customize your home screen 25

Application icon 26

background 26

Theme 27

Symbol 28

Easy mode 29

Status Bar 30

Notification icons 30

Configure status bar display options...................31

Notification panel...31

View notification panel 32

Quick Setup 32

Quick settings options..33

Bixby 35

Camera 36

Gallery..36

Internet 37

Modes and Routines 37

Digital wellbeing and parental controls 38

Chapter Two 41

Biometric security 41

Fingerprint scanner 43

Fingerprint management 44

Fingerprint verification settings........................... 44

Biometric settings.. 45

Multi-window... 46

Window control... 47

Edge board 47

Application panel 48

Configure the application panel.......................... 49

Chapter Three... 50

Camera and gallery 50

Camera 50

Navigate camera screen 51

Gallery.. 52

Custom image and video collections 53

View pictures 53

Edit picture 54

Apps.. 56

Utilizing mobile applications............................... 56

Contact 58

Create contact 58

Edit contact... 59

Share contacts... 59

Internet..60

    Tabs within a web browser 60

    Create a bookmark for your reading pleasure.......61

    Open a Bookmark...61

    Save a webpage...61

Messages 63

    Searching for messages.......................................64

    Remove all discussions 64

    Urgent communication 65

My file 66

    File group 66

    My file settings...67

Chapter Four 68

Phone..68

    Calls...69

    Place a phone call..69

    Respond to a phone call......................................70

    Reject an incoming phone call 71

    Send a message to express your decline...............71

    Operations during a call 72

    Switch to headphones or speakers 72

    Multitasking..73

    Return to the call screen.....................................73

To end a call while multitasking 73

Call background 73

Open popup settings 73

Manage calls...74

Call records 74

Save contacts from recent calls.........................75

Delete call recording..75

Block number 76

Speed Dial...76

Make a call using speed dial 77

Delete speed dial number 77

Emergency call..78

Cellphone setting..78

Chapter Five 79

S Pen 79

Taking out the S Pen from its slot 79

Air view 80

Air operations 81

Press and hold a keyboard shortcut on the S Pen 81

Action in everywhere..82

Application operations 83

General application operations............................83

Screen off memo...83

Fixed to always-on display.................................. 84

Air command 84

NFC and payment 87

Conveniently make purchases with a simple tap of
your device 88

Lock screen and security 89

Different types of screen locks 89

Set a secure screen lock 89

Restore factory settings password 92

Set up SIM card lock.. 92

Show password 93

Reset to default 93

Reset all settings 93

Reset network settings... 93

Reset accessibility settings 94

Reset.. 94

Before resetting your device 95

To reset your device 95

INTRODUCTION

The User Guide for the Samsung Galaxy S24 Ultra 5G is an interactive and informative resource designed to optimize your device usage. Whether you're a novice or an expert in mobile technology, this crucial tool equips you with the knowledge and proficiency required to efficiently navigate your device. Delve into this comprehensive guide to explore the multifaceted capabilities of the Samsung Galaxy S24 Ultra 5G, uncovering invaluable tips and tricks along the way.

Your device set up

Your device or smartphone uses a Nano SIM card. The SIM card may be preinstalled, or you can use an existing SIM card. Network metrics for 5G services are based on your service provider's specifications and network availability. You can call your service provider for further detail.

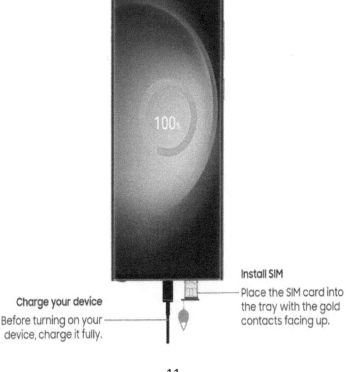

Install SIM
Place the SIM card into the tray with the gold contacts facing up.

Charge your device
Before turning on your device, charge it fully.

Notice: Your device has an IP68 dust and water resistance rating. To maintain the water and dust resistance of your device, please be right ensure that your device SIM card tray opening is free of dust and water and that the tray is firmly inserted before coming into contact with liquids.

Chapter One
On your device

Basically, use the side button to turn on your device. Please do not use the device if the casing is cracked or damaged. Only use the device after it has been repaired.

- Press and hold down the side button to on the device.

- To off the device, simply press ⏻ and hold down the Side button and Volume Down button simultaneously, then click on Power off. You can confirm when prompted.

- To resume or restart your device, press ⏻ and hold down the Side button and Volume Down button simultaneously, then click on Restart. You can confirm when prompted.

Notice: For optimal 5G performance, an optimal 5G connection and a free antenna (back of device) are required. For network availability, please contact your service provider. 5G performance may be affected by the case or cover.

Use the setup wizard

When you turn on your device for the first time, a setup wizard walks you through the basics of setting up your device.

Follow the instructions to choose your default language, connect to a Wi-Fi® network, set up your account, choose location services, learn more about your device's features, and more.

Get data from old devices

Download and install Smart Switch™ to move contacts, pictures, music, films, messages, notes, calendars, and a lot from your previous device. Smart switches can also transmit your data via USB cable, WiFi or computer.

1. In Settings, tap Accounts & backup > Transfer data from old device.

2. Follow the instructions and select what you want to transfer.

Lock or unlock your device

Protect your device using its screen lock feature. By default, the device automatically locks when the screen expires. For more information about screen lock, see Screen lock and security.

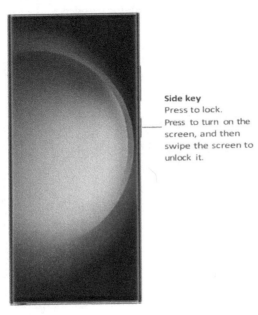

Side key
Press to lock.
Press to turn on the screen, and then swipe the screen to unlock it.

Side button settings

You can customize the keyboard shortcuts assigned to the side buttons.

Click twice

Choose the function that activates when you press the side button twice.

1. In Settings, tap ⊕ Advanced features > Side buttons.

2. Tap "Double tap" to activate this feature, then tap the options: Quick launch camera (default) Open application

Press and hold

Choose the features that activate when you hold down the side button.

1. In Settings, tap ⊕ Advanced features > Side buttons.

2. In the Press and hold heading, click an option:

- Open Bixby (default)
- Close the menu.

Account

Set up and manage your account.

TIP: Accounts may support email, calendaring, contacts, and other features.

Add google account

Sign in to your Google Account to access your Google Cloud storage and apps installed from your account, and take advantage of your device's Android™ features.

Google Device Protection is activated when you sign in to your Google Account and set your lock screen. This service requires your Google Account information when performing a factory reset.

1. In Settings, click ⟳ Accounts & backup > Manage account.

2. Click ✛ Add account > Google.

Add Samsung account

Sign in to your Samsung account to access exclusive Samsung content and make the most of Samsung apps.

- Click "Samsung Account" in "Settings".

Add Outlook account

To view and manage email and you can sign in to your Outlook® account.

1. In Settings, click ⟳ Accounts & backup > Manage account.

2. Click ✛ Add Account > Outlook.

Set up voicemail

You can set up your voicemail service the first time you access it. Through the telephone application and you can also access voicemail.

1. In your phone, touch and hold key 1 or tap Voicemail.

2. Follow the instructions to create a password, record a greeting, and record your name.

navigation

Touch screens respond best to light touches from your fingertips or capacitive stylus. Applying excessive force or metal objects to the touch screen may damage the screen surface and such damage is not covered by the warranty.

Press

Tap items to select or launch them.

- Click an item to select it.
- Double-click the image to zoom in or out.

Swipe

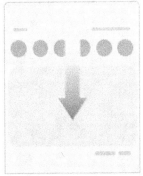

Drag your finger gently across the screen.

- To unlock your telephone carefully swipe the screen.

- Kindly swipe the screen to easily scroll over the home screen or menu selections.

Drag and drop

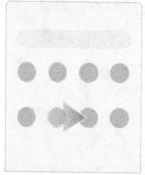

Press and simply hold an item, then transfer it to a new place.

- Drag an application shortcut to add it to the home screen.
- Pull the widget to station it in a new place.

Zoom in and out

Move your thumb and index finger together or apart on the screen to zoom in and out.

- Spread your thumb and index finger on the screen to zoom in.

- Move your thumb and index finger on the screen simultaneously to zoom out.

Touch and hold

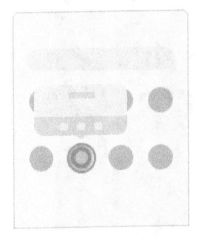

Touch and hold items to activate them.

- Do press and hold a field to show the pop-up menu of selections.

- Long press the home screen to customize the home screen.

Navigation Bar

You can use the navigation keys or gestures to navigate your device in full-screen mode.

Recent apps

Back

Home

Navigation buttons

Use the buttons at the bottom of the screen for quick navigation.

1. In Settings, click Display > Navigation Bar > Buttons.

2. Under Key sequence, tap an option to choose which side of the screen the Back and Recent Apps icons appear.

Navigation gestures

Navigation gestures have become increasingly popular among smartphone users. Rather than utilizing physical buttons, these gestures allow users to navigate their devices using different swipes and taps. With the rise of bezel-less displays and larger screens, navigation gestures provide a more immersive experience, allowing users to maximize their screen space. Additionally, these gestures can increase efficiency and speed of navigation for those who prefer them over traditional buttons.

For an uninterrupted viewing experience, it is recommended that you hide the navigation buttons located at the bottom of your screen. This will allow for unobstructed access to the entirety of the display. Instead, utilize swiping gestures to navigate your device.

1. To activate the feature, navigate to Settings and select the Display option.

2. From there, click on Navigation bar and then Swipe gestures. This will allow you to use the swipe feature.

-   More options: You have the option to select from a variety of gesture types and levels of sensitivity.

-   The screen can display lines at the bottom, providing a gesture cue for users.

-   The act of making a gesture is defined by its placement or position.

-   ✓ Enabling the "Switch apps when hint hidden" option allows you to switch between apps using the gesture even when the gesture hint is disabled. This feature allows for seamless switching between apps without the need for a visual cue.

- To allow for the hiding of the keyboard when a device is in portrait mode, a button should be shown on the bottom right corner of the screen. This button would provide an easy and convenient way for users to access the full screen and enhance their experience.

- If you are an owner of a Galaxy S24, you can prevent the S Pen from executing navigation gestures by using the block gesture feature.

Customize your home screen

The home screen is the initial point for piloting your device automatically. Here you can place your favorite apps and widgets, set up additional home screens, delete screens, change the order of screens, and select a primary home screen.

Application icon

Launch apps from any home screen using the app icon.

- Under Apps, touch and hold the app icon, then click ⌂ Add to Home.

To remove an icon:

- On the Home screen, touch and hold the app icon, then tap 🗑 Delete.

  Notice: That deleting an icon does not delete the app, it just removes the icon from the home screen.

background

Change the look of your home and lock screens by choosing your favorite images, videos, or preinstalled wallpapers.

1. In the Home screen, touch and hold the screen, then click 🖼 Wallpapers & styles.

2. Click on one of the following menus to view available wallpapers:

- Tap lock screen and home screen images to edit them.

- Change wallpaper: Choose from various wallpaper options or download more wallpapers from Galaxy Theme.

- Palette: Choose a color palette based on the colors of the background image.

- Darken wallpaper when dark mode is enabled: Enable this option to apply dark mode to the wallpaper.

Theme

Set themes for your home and lock screens, wallpapers, and app icons.

1. On the Home screen, touch and hold the screen.

2. Click ⬚ on the theme, then click on the theme to preview and download.

3. Click ≣ Menu > My Profile > Themes to view downloaded themes.

4. Click a theme, then click Apply to apply the selected theme.

Symbol

Apply a different icon set to replace the default icons.

1. On the Home screen, touch and hold the screen.

2. Click ⌻ Theme > Icons, then click the icon set you want to preview and download.

3. Click ☰ Menu > My Profile > Icons to view the downloaded icons.

4. Click an icon, then click Apply to apply the selected icon set.

Easy mode

The simple mode layout features larger text and icons for a simpler visual experience. Switch between standard screen layout and simpler layout.

1. In "Settings" click  Show > Easy mode.

2. Click  to activate this feature. The following options are displayed:

- Touch and hold delay: Set the time required for consecutive touches to be recognized as touch and hold.

- High-contrast keyboard: You can pick a keyboard with the most high-contrast colors.

Device information is available on the right side of the status bar, and notifications are available on the left.

Status Bar

| Battery full | Charging | Mute | Vibrate |
| Airplane mode | Bluetooth active | Location active | Alarm |

Notification icons

| Missed calls | Call in progress | New message | Voicemail |
| New email | Download | Upload | App update |

Configure status bar display options

Tip: In quick settings, tap :More options > Status bar to configure status bar notification settings.

Notification panel

For quick access to notifications, settings, and more, just open the notification panel.

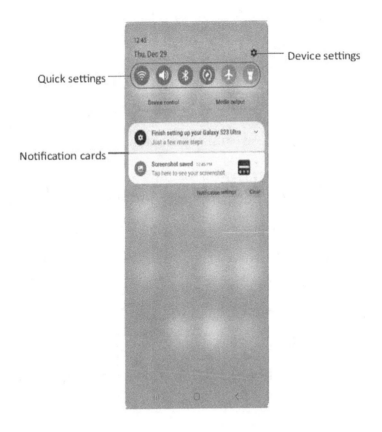

Quick settings

Device settings

Notification cards

View notification panel

You can access the notification panel from any screen.

1. Swipe down the screen to display the notification panel.

- To open an item, click on it.
- To delete an individual notification, drag the notification left or right.
- To clear all notifications, tap Clear.
- To customize notifications, tap Notification settings.

2. Drag up from the bottom of the screen or tap Return to close Notification panel.

Quick Setup

The notification panel provides quick access to device features through quick settings. The following icons show the most commonly used settings in Quick Settings. The icon color changes when enabled and disabled. There may be other settings available on your device.

1. To show the Notification panel drag the Status bar down.

2.   To show Quick settings swipe down from the top of the screen.

- Touch a quick setting icon to activate it on or off.

- Press and hold down a quick setting icon to start the setting.

| Wi-Fi | Sound | Bluetooth | Auto rotate |
| Airplane mode | Location | Power saving | Dark mode |

Quick settings options

The options for quick settings can be accessed with ease and swiftness. These options allow users to alter various settings on their devices, such as Wi-Fi connectivity, volume, screen brightness, and airplane mode. They are designed to be convenient and easily accessible, providing users with shortcuts to frequently used options and settings.

Quick settings offer a variety of options for users to choose from.

Finder: The finder application is designed to facilitate the searching of files and data on the device.

Power off: The available options for power management on this device include both powering off and restarting.

Accessing the settings menu of the device can be done swiftly.

More options: There are additional choices available for users, such as the ability to modify the layout of the Quick settings or rearrange the order of buttons.

- One can control other devices with ease by utilizing supported applications such as SmartThings or Google Home, granting access to the feature of device control.

- To manage playback of connected audio and video devices, users can utilize the Media panel. This feature provides access to media output control.

- The slider for brightness can be found on your screen, and by dragging it you can modify the light level of your display.

Bixby

Bixby functions as a digital assistant that has the ability to learn, develop, and conform to your specific needs. As you use it more regularly, it begins to understand your routines and habits, assisting you in setting reminders based on both your current location and the time of day. It also has the added convenience of being integrated into your most frequently used applications.

To access the Home screen on your device, simply press and hold the Side key until it appears.

Bixby can be accessed through the Apps list as well.

Bixby Vision is an advanced feature that allows for the identification of objects, translation of text, and scanning of QR codes through the camera of a Samsung smartphone.

Your Camera, Gallery, and Internet apps are seamlessly integrated with Bixby, allowing for a more comprehensive comprehension of visual content. The program offers contextualized icons for a variety of functions such as QR code scanning, translation, recognition of iconic landmarks, and shopping.

Camera

To aid in comprehending one's surroundings, the Camera viewfinder now offers Bixby Vision.

To access Bixby Vision on your Camera app, simply tap the "More" button and follow the prompts provided.

Gallery

The application known as Bixby Vision has the capability to function with visual content that has been preserved within the Gallery app, including both pictures and images.

1. To view a picture on Gallery, simply tap on the desired image.

2. To initiate the Bixby Vision feature, simply tap on the corresponding icon and proceed with the instructions that appear.

Internet

When browsing through the Internet app, Bixby Vision has the ability to provide you with additional information about any image you may come across.

1. To retrieve an image from the internet, press and hold on the image until a menu appears.

2. To use Bixby Vision's search function, simply tap on the "Search" option and follow the prompts provided.

Modes and Routines

Modes and routines refer to the habitual patterns of behavior and thought that we establish in our daily lives. These can encompass a wide range of activities; from the way we organize our morning routines to the way we approach problem-solving at work. Our modes and routines are often deeply ingrained, and can be difficult to change without a conscious effort to do so. However, by recognizing and analyzing our modes and routines, we can gain greater control over our lives and make more intentional decisions about how we want to live.

To access the designated pages, navigate to the Settings app, then select ⊘ "Modes and Routines". This option can be found by tapping on it from the main menu.

- Modes: Select a mode based on where you are or what you are doing.
- Routines: Create or make phone routines based on times or areas.

Digital wellbeing and parental controls

The concept of digital wellbeing and parental controls go hand in hand to ensure a safe and healthy online experience for users of all ages.

To effectively oversee and regulate your digital routines, it is possible to obtain a daily overview of your app usage frequency, notification count, and device check frequency. Additionally, you have the ability to configure your device to assist in winding down before bedtime.

To access the desired features, navigate to the Settings menu and tap on ⊙ Digital Wellbeing and parental controls.

To access the following information, simply tap on the Dashboard.

Monitor the duration and usage of an app on a daily basis by tracking screen time.

Keep track of the number of notifications received from an app on a daily basis by viewing the notification count.

Gain insight into the daily usage of an app by tracking the number of times it has been opened and unlocked.

Establish a specific screen time objective and monitor your average daily screen usage.

You have the ability to set a daily time restriction for the usage of each individual app with the help of app timers.

With the driving monitor feature, you can keep track of your screen time by connecting to your car's Bluetooth and easily identify the most frequently used apps.

- Volume monitor: To keep your ears safe select a sound source to observe the volume.

- Parental controls: Monitor your children's digital life with Google's Family Link application. You can also pick applications and by setting the content filters, keep an eye on screen time, and also set limits for the screen time.

Chapter Two
Biometric security

The implementation of biometric security measures has become increasingly prevalent in recent years.

Employ the use of biometrics as a secure means to unlock your device and gain access to various accounts.

The procedure of recognizing persons based on their facial structures.

To gain access to your device, you have the option to activate Face Recognition as a means of unlocking your screen. However, in order to utilize this feature, it is necessary to establish a pattern, PIN, or password.

Pattern, PIN, or Password are more secure methods of authentication compared to face recognition. It is possible for your device to be unlocked by someone or something that bears a resemblance to your image.

The recognition of faces can be influenced by various factors such as the presence of glasses, hats, beards, or heavy make-up.

Make sure you are in a well-lit environment and that the camera lens is free from dirt when registering your face.

To access the Face recognition feature, navigate to Settings and then tap on 🔘 Security and privacy, followed by Biometrics.

Register your face by following the provided prompts.

The management of face recognition technology and systems.

Modify the functionality of facial recognition to meet your specific needs.

In Settings, tap 🔘 Security & Privacy > Biometrics > Facial Recognition.

- Delete face data: Delete existing faces.

- Add alternative appearances for improved recognition: Improve facial recognition by adding alternative appearances.

- Face Unlock: Enable or disable facial recognition security.

- Stay on lock screen until swipe: When you unlock your device with facial recognition, you stay on lock screen until you swipe.

- Eyes open required: Face detection only recognizes your face when your eyes are open.

- Brighten screen: Temporarily increase screen brightness so your face can be recognized in the dark.

- About facial recognition: Learn more about securing your device with facial recognition.

Fingerprint scanner

Use fingerprint recognition as an alternative to entering passwords in some applications.

You can also use your fingerprint to verify your identity when you log into your Samsung account. To unlock your device with your fingerprint, you need to set up a pattern, PIN, or password.

1. In Settings, tap ⬤ Security & Privacy > Biometrics > Fingerprint.

2. Follow the instructions to register your fingerprint.

Fingerprint management

Add, delete and rename fingerprints.

- In Settings, tap ⬤ Security & Privacy > Biometrics > Fingerprint to see the following options:

- The list of registered fingerprints is at the top of the list. You can click on the fingerprint to delete or rename it.

- Add a fingerprint: Simply follow the instructions to register another fingerprint.

- Checking the added fingerprints: Kindly scan your fingerprint to observe if it has been registered.

Fingerprint verification settings

You can use the fingerprint recognition to confirm your identity in supported applications and activities.

- In Settings, tap ⬤ Security & Privacy > Biometrics > Fingerprint.

- Unlocking Fingerprint: You can use your fingerprint for identification when you intend to unlock your device.

- Always on Fingerprint: You can also scan your fingerprint even when the screen is shutdown.

- Show icon when screen is off: Display the fingerprint icon when the screen is off.

- Show animation when unlocking: Show animation when using fingerprint verification.

- About fingerprints: Learn more about protecting your device with fingerprints.

Biometric settings

Configure your biometric security option preferences.

- In Settings, tap ⬤ Security & Privacy > Biometrics to do the following:

- Show unlock transition: Show a transition when you unlock your device using biometrics.

- About unlocking using biometrics: Learn more about using biometrics to secure your device.

Multi-window

Multitask using multiple apps at the same time. Applications that support Multi Window™ can be displayed together on split screen. You can switch between applications and resize their windows.

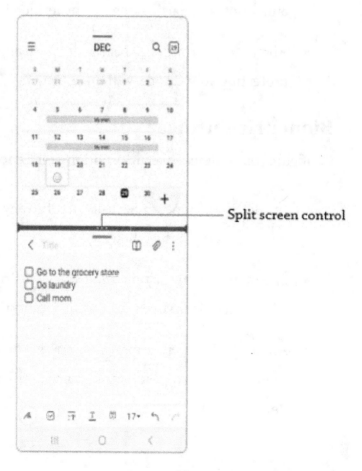

Split screen control

1. Tap ||| Recent Apps on any screen.

2. Tap the app icon, then tap Open in split-screen view.

3. In another window, tap an app to add it to split-screen view.

- Drag the center of the window edge to resize the window.

Window control

Window controls change how application windows appear in split-screen view.

1. Drag the center of the window edge to resize the window.

2. Click in the center of the edge of the window to display the following options:

- ↑↓ Switch Window: Swap two windows.

- ☆ Add app pair to: Create an app pair shortcut and add it to the app panel on the Edge screen.

Edge board

Edge Panels feature a variety of customizable panels accessible from the edges of the screen. The Edge panel lets you access apps, tasks, and contacts, as well as view news, sports, and other information.

○ In Settings, click 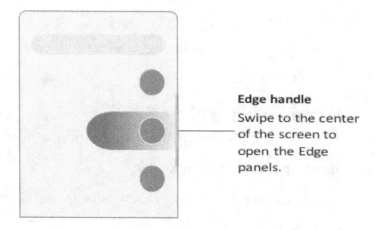 Display > Borders, then tap

to enable this feature.

Edge handle
Swipe to the center of the screen to open the Edge panels.

Application panel

You can add applications to the Applications section.

1. On any screen, drag an edge handle to the center of the screen. Slide until the Applications window appears.

2. Click an application or application pair shortcut to open it. Do click ⋮⋮⋮ "All Apps" to get a whole list of applications.

- To open other windows in pop-up view, drag the application icon from the application area to the open screen.

Configure the application panel

1. On any screen, drag an edge handle to the center of the screen. Slide until the Applications window appears.

2. Click Edit to add more apps to the Apps section.

- To add an app to the Apps section, find the app on the left side of the screen and tap it to add it to the available space in the right column.

- To generate a folder shortcut, pull an application in between the left side of the screen on upper of an application in the columns on the right.

- To transform the order of the applications on the panel, pull each application to the favorite location.

- To delete an app, click Remove.

3. Click on the Back to save changes.

Chapter Three
Camera and gallery

The camera app allows you to capture high-quality images and videos. Images and videos are saved in the gallery where you can view and edit them.

Camera

Enjoy a full suite of professional lenses and professional video modes and settings.

- Under Apps, tap Camera.

Tip: Press the side button twice quickly to open the Camera app.

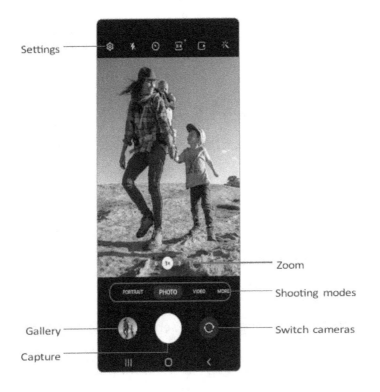

Settings

Zoom

Shooting modes

Gallery

Switch cameras

Capture

Navigate camera screen

Take stunning photos using your device's front and back cameras.

1. In the 📷 camera, set up recording using the following functions:

- Tap the screen you want the camera to focus on.
- ✓ When you tap the screen, the brightness level appears. Drag the slider to adjust brightness.

- To quickly switch between the front and back cameras, swipe up or down on the screen.

- To zoom to a precise level, tap 1x, then tap Options at the bottom of the screen. (Available only when using the rear camera.)

- To switch to another shooting mode, swipe the screen to the right or left.

- To change camera settings, click ⚙ Settings.

2. Click ⭕ Capture.

Gallery

Go to the Gallery to view all visual media stored on your device. You can view, edit and manage images and videos.

- Under Applications, click ✳ Gallery.

Custom image and video collections

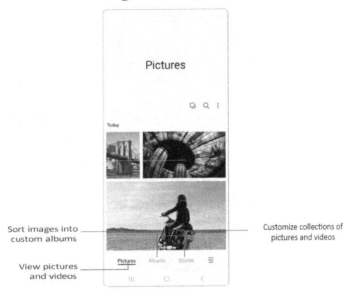

Sort images into custom albums

Customize collections of pictures and videos

View pictures and videos

View pictures

Images stored on your device can be viewed in the Gallery app.

1. In the ✱ Gallery, do click on an image.

2. Click on the image to view it. Swipe left or right to view additional images or videos.

- To use Bixby Vision with the current image, click 👁 Bixby Vision. For more information, see Bixby.

- To mark an image as a favorite, click ♡ Add to Favorites.

- To access the following features, click ⋮ More options:

✓ Details: View and edit information about the image.

✓ Remaster images: Optimize images using automatic image enhancements.

✓ Add Portrait Effect: Increase or decrease the visibility of the background in your portrait photo by dragging the slider.

✓ Copy to clipboard: Copy the image to paste it into another application.

✓ Set as wallpaper: Image can be set as wallpaper.

Edit picture

Enhance your images with gallery editing tools.

1. In the 🌼 Gallery do click on an image.

2. Click the image to view it, then click ◇ Edit to display the following options:

- ☀ Auto Adjustment: Apply automatic adjustments to improve the image.

- ⟳ Transform: Rotate, flip, crop, or make other changes to the overall appearance of the image.

- ◌ Filter: Add color effects.

- ☼ Sound: Adjust brightness, exposure, contrast, etc.

- ☺ Decorate: Add text, stickers or hand-drawn content.

- ⋮ More options: Access additional editing features.

- Reset: Undo the changes you made to restore the original image.

3. Click Save when finished.

Apps

Utilizing mobile applications

All preloaded and downloaded apps are conveniently listed in the Apps list. Users have the option to download apps from both the Galaxy Store and the Google Play™ store.

To access the Apps list, simply swipe the screen upwards from the Home screen.

You have the option to either uninstall or disable applications on your device.

You have the ability to uninstall apps that have been installed on your device. However, there are certain preloaded apps that come with your device and cannot be completely removed; they can only be disabled. When an app is disabled, it is deactivated and no longer visible in the Apps list.

To remove or disable an app, simply touch and hold the desired app on your device's screen, then select the Uninstall/Disable option.

Explore the wide array of applications available for your search.

In case you are uncertain about the location of an application or a specific setting, you can utilize the Search feature to assist you.

To search for a specific app or setting, begin by tapping on "Apps." Then, enter the desired word or words in the search bar. As you type, the screen will display relevant results, including matching apps and settings.

To access a specific app, simply tap on the desired result.

To personalize the search preferences, simply tap on ⋮ More options and then navigate to the Settings section.

Contact

Save and manage your contacts. You can sync with personal accounts added to your device. Accounts can also support email, calendaring, and other features.

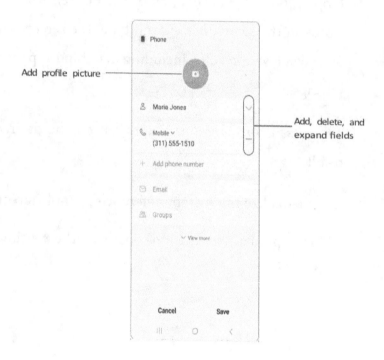

Add profile picture

Add, delete, and expand fields

Create contact

1. In 👤 "Contacts", click ➕ "Create Contact".

2. Input the contact information and click on Save.

Edit contact

When editing a contact, you can click on a field and change or delete the information, or you can add additional fields to the contact's information list.

1. Click 🔘 a contact under Contacts.

2. Click ✏️ Edit.

3. Click any field to add, change, or delete information.

4. Click Save.

Share contacts

Share contacts with others using a variety of sharing methods and services.

1. Click 🔘 a contact under Contacts.

2. Click ⌁ Share.

3. Click on the vCard file (VCF) or text.

4. Select how to share and follow the instructions.

Tip: While viewing contacts, tap ⋮ More > QR Code to quickly share information with friends or family. When you change the contact information fields, the QR code updates automatically.

Internet

Enhance your browsing experience with Samsung Internet, a web browser that is not only simple and fast but also reliable. Enjoy the benefits of more secure web browsing features that not only allow for faster browsing but also protect your privacy.

Tabs within a web browser

To simultaneously view multiple webpages, employ the use of tabs.

To open a new tab, simply tap 🔲 on the "Tabs" option

and then select 🔲 "New tab" from the menu in your

⬤ Internet browser.

In order to close a tab, simply tap 🔲 on the "Tabs"

option and select ⊗ "Close tab".

Create a bookmark for your reading pleasure

- To conveniently access your preferred

  webpages, make sure to ☆ bookmark them.

Open a Bookmark

1. To save the currently open webpage, simply tap

   ☆ on "Add to bookmarks" from within the ⬤

   Internet browser.

2. Preserve the contents of a webpage.

Save a webpage

Within the Samsung Internet app, users have multiple choices available to them when it comes to saving a webpage.

- To access additional options, simply tap ☰ on the Tools icon located in the 🌐 Internet app, and then select "Add page to" from the menu.

- Bookmarks: Include the webpage in your list of bookmarks for easy access in the future.

- Quick access: Effortlessly retrieve frequently visited or bookmarked webpages through quick access.

- Home screen: On your Home screen, you can conveniently create a shortcut to the webpage for easy access.

- Saved pages: By saving webpages on your device, you can conveniently access their content even without an internet connection.

Messages

Stay connected with your acquaintances through the Messages application, where you can exchange pictures, express yourself with emojis, or simply send a brief greeting. The available features may differ depending on your service provider.

- In 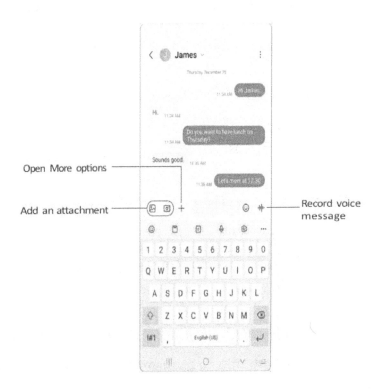Messages, click ♀ write new message.

Searching for messages

For efficient message retrieval, utilize the search function to swiftly locate the desired information.

1. To access the search function, navigate to the Messages app and tap on the Search option.

2. To initiate a search, input relevant keywords into the designated Search field and proceed to tap the Search button on the keyboard.

Remove all discussions

To eliminate your conversion history, simply delete the conversations.

1. To delete a message, simply tap on More options and select Delete.

2. To delete specific conversations, simply tap on each one individually.

3. Select the option to Delete all, and follow the prompts to confirm your decision.

Urgent communication

Ensure that your emergency contacts receive a message containing both pictures and audio.

- To initiate the specified actions, simply tap on

  Safety and emergency in the Settings menu, followed by Emergency SOS. By enabling this feature, you can activate the desired functions by pressing the Side key five times.

- Countdown: Select the desired duration in seconds for initiating emergency measures.

- In the event of an emergency, select the appropriate number to dial for immediate assistance.

My file

You can view and manage all files that are downloaded and stored on your device, such as images, videos, music, and sound clips. You can also access and manage files stored in your cloud account.

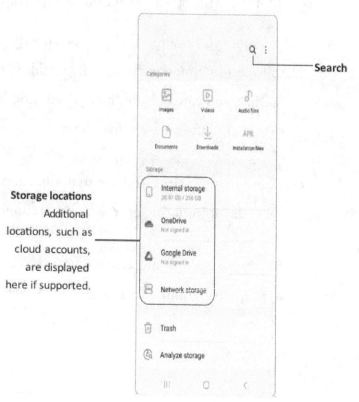

Search

Storage locations
Additional locations, such as cloud accounts, are displayed here if supported.

File group

Files stored on the device are divided into the following groups:

- Recent files: View recently accessed files.
- ✓ This option appears when one or more files have been recently accessed.
- Category: View files based on their type.
- Storage: View files stored on your device and cloud account.
- ✓ Cloud accounts vary depending on the service you log into.
- Analyze storage: See what content is taking up storage space.

My file settings

Use My Files to set custom file management options and more.

- In My ⬭ Files, click ⋮ More Options > Settings to see the following options:
- Cloud Account: Connect and manage your cloud services.
- File management: Customize how files are viewed and deleted, and how you access mobile data.

Chapter Four
Phone

Beyond its primary function of making phone calls, the Phone app offers a range of advanced calling features. For further details, reach out to your service provider. It's important to note that the appearance and available options on the Phone app screen may differ depending on your specific service provider.

Calls

With the Phone app, users have the convenience of making and receiving calls directly from various sections such as the Home screen, Recents tab, Contacts, and more.

Place a phone call

Utilize your mobile device to initiate and respond to phone calls directly from the Home screen.

- To make a call, simply enter a number on the keypad of your phone and tap the call button.

If the keypad is not visible, you can tap on the keypad to display it.

Place a phone call using the "Recents" section of your device.

The Call log keeps a record of all incoming, outgoing, and missed calls that have occurred.

1. To view a record of your recent phone calls, simply tap on the Recents option on your device. This will provide you with a

comprehensive list of all the calls you have made or received.

2. To initiate a 📞 phone call, simply select a contact and tap on it.

Initiate a phone call by selecting a contact from your list of saved contacts.

Make a phone call to a contact stored in the Contacts application.

- To initiate a call, simply swipe your finger to the right across a contact in the 👤 Contacts section.

Respond to a phone call

Upon receiving a call, the phone will ring and promptly display the caller's name or phone number. When utilizing an application, a screen will appear as a pop-up when there is an incoming call.

- To answer the call, simply swipe the 📞 Answer option to the right on the incoming call screen.

To answer an incoming call, simply tap on the 📞 Answer option displayed on the pop-up screen.

Reject an incoming phone call

When an incoming call comes through, you have the option to reject it. In the case of using an application, a screen will appear, presenting a pop-up for the incoming call.

- To reject an incoming call and direct it to your voicemail, simply drag the "Decline" option towards the left on the call screen.

When the pop-up screen appears, simply tap on the Decline option to reject the call and redirect it to your voicemail.

Send a message to express your decline

When an incoming call comes in, you have the option to decline it and respond with a text message instead.

- To send a message on the incoming call screen, simply drag the "Send message" option upwards and choose a message to send.

Tip: To send a message on the incoming call pop-up screen, simply tap on "Send message" and choose a message from the options provided.

Terminate the ongoing phone conversation.

- When you are finished with your call, simply tap on the ⬤ "End Call" option.

Operations during a call

You can adjust call volume, switch to headphones or speakers, and even multitask during a call.

- Press the volume button up and down to bring up or bring down the volume.

Switch to headphones or speakers

Answer calls via speakerphone or Bluetooth headset (not included).

- Click 🔊 "Speaker" to hear the caller's voice through the speaker, or click ᛓ "Bluetooth" to hear the caller's voice through the Bluetooth headset.

Multitasking

When you leave the call screen to use another app, the current call appears in the status bar.

Return to the call screen

- Drag the status bar down to display the notification panel and tap Call.

To end a call while multitasking

- Drag the status bar downward to display the notification panel, then tap 🔴 End Call.

Call background

Select an image or video to display when making or receiving calls.

On your 🅖 phone, tap ⋮ More options > Settings > Call background to view the following options:

- Layout: Choose how caller information is displayed when someone has a profile photo.

- Wallpaper: Select a photo to display during calls.

Open popup settings

If calls come in while using other apps, they may appear as pop-ups.

- On your ⓒ phone, while using the app, tap More Options > Settings > Caller ID. The following options are available:

- Full screen: Show incoming calls in full screen phone app.

- Small pop-up window: Displays incoming calls as a pop-up window at the top of the screen.

- Mini pop-up: Display incoming calls as smaller pop-ups.

- Keep call in pop-up window: Enable this option to keep the call-in pop-up window after answering.

Manage calls

Your calls are recorded in the call log. Setting up speed dials, block numbers, and use voicemail is also allowed.

Call records

Phone numbers you dial, answer, or miss are saved in the call history.

Under 📞 "Phone," click "Recents." Display the recent calls list. If the caller is in your contact list, the caller's name will displayed.

Save contacts from recent calls

Create contacts or update your contact list with recent call information.

1. Under 📞 Phone, tap Recent Calls.

2. Tap the call that contains the information you want to save to your contact list, and then tap Add to Contacts.

3. Tap to create a new contact or update an existing contact.

Delete call recording

To delete call log entries:

1. Under 📞 Phone, tap Recent Calls.

2. Press and hold the call you want to delete from the call history.

3. Click 🗑 Delete.

Block number

If you add a caller to your block list, future calls from that number will go directly to your voicemail and no messages will be received.

1. Under 🅒 Phone, tap Recent Calls.

2. Tap your desire caller to add to the block list, and then click on the ⓘ Details.

3. Click on the ⊘ Block or ⁝ More > Block Contact and check on it when prompted.

Tip: You can also change your block list in Settings. On your phone, tap ⁝ More options > Settings > Block number.

Speed Dial

You can assign speed dial numbers to contacts to quickly dial their default number.

1. On your 🅒 phone, tap Keyboard > ⁝ More options > Speed dial numbers. The reserved speed dial number appears on the Speed Dial Numbers screen.

2. Click on an unassigned number.

- Click ▼ Menu to select a speed dial number in addition to the next sequence.

- Number 1 is reserved for voicemail.

3. Enter a name or number, or click ♟Add from Contacts to assign a contact to the number.

- The selected contact appears in the Speed Dial Number field.

Make a call using speed dial

You can use speed dial to make calls.

- On your 🅒 phone, touch and hold the speed dial number.

- If the speed dial number is longer than one digit, enter the first few digits and then press and hold the last digit.

Delete speed dial number

You can delete assigned speed dial numbers.

1. Under 🅒 Phone, click ⋮ More options > Speed dial numbers.

2. Tap ▬ Delete next to the contact you want to remove from speed dial.

Emergency call

You can call emergency numbers in your area regardless of your phone's service status. If your phone is not activated, you can only make emergency calls.

1. Under 🅒 Phone, enter the emergency number (911 in North America) and click Call.

2. End the call. During this type of call, you can use most call features.

Tips Emergency numbers can be dialed even when your phone is locked, so anyone can use your phone to call for help in an emergency. Callers can only use the emergency calling feature when accessed from the lock screen. The rest of the phone remains secure.

Cellphone setting

These settings allow you to change settings associated with the Phone application.

- In your 🅒 telephone, click on the ⦙ More options > Settings.

Chapter Five
S Pen

The S Pen provides a multitude of practical features. Whether it's opening apps, creating artwork, or jotting down notes, the S Pen is your go-to tool. However, please note that certain S Pen functions, like touchscreen tapping (exclusive to the Galaxy S24 Ultra), may not work properly if your phone is close to a magnet.

S Pen button

Taking out the S Pen from its slot

For convenient accessibility, the S Pen is kept at the bottom of your device. Additionally, your device charges the S Pen so that it can be utilized for remote functions.

To remove the S Pen, simply press it inward and then slide it out.

Please ensure that the S Pen slot and opening remain dry and clean, and that the pen is securely inserted before exposing your device to liquids, in order to protect its water and dust resistance capabilities.

Air view

Utilize the S Pen to effortlessly access information or preview content on your screen. Take advantage of the various Air viewing features at your disposal.

- Preview an email before opening it.

- Preview album content/enlarge the image.

- Preview videos and navigate to specific scenes by hovering your mouse over the timeline.

- Display the name/description/ of any symbol button.

Notice: The preview feature is only available when the S Pen's on-screen pointer is a solid color.

Air operations

You can use the S Pen to set shortcuts to your favorite apps, perform actions, navigate your device screen, and more. You can also use the S Pen's buttons and gestures or movements to perform remote functions.

Only Samsung-approved S Pens with Bluetooth Low Energy (BLE) functionality can use the S Pen remote control feature. Your S Pen will disconnect from any device if it's too far away or if there's interference. For flight operation, the S Pen must be connected.

- Under the "Settings", click on the "Advanced features" > then choose "S Pen" > and then "Air Action" to activate this feature.

Press and hold a keyboard shortcut on the S Pen

You can set shortcuts by holding down the S Pen button. This option is set to open your camera app by default.

1. Click on the "Advanced features" in "Settings" > click on the "S Pen" > and pick "Air Operations".

2. Click and hold the pen button. Then click ⬭ to activate the feature.

Action in everywhere

If you hold down the S Pen button while performing any of these gestures, you can access configurable shortcuts called Any Actions: down, up, right, left, or by shaking. This includes apps, S Pen functionality and navigation accessible from any screen.

Back left to right

Resents right to left

Home down and up

Smart selecting up and down

Screen writing zigzag

1. In Settings, click ✦ Advanced features > and select S Pen > Air Actions.

2. Tap any gesture icon under "Actions from Anywhere" to customize the shortcut.

Application operations

Your S Pen can be used for specific actions in specific apps.

1. Click on the ⚙ "Advanced features" in "Settings"> and pick the "S Pen" > "Air Operations".

2. Tap any app to see available shortcuts.

3. Tap ⬤ to activate your shortcut while using this app.

General application operations

If you're using a camera or media app that's not on the list of app actions, you can customize some common actions.

1. In Settings, click ⚙ Advanced features > S Pen > Air Actions.

2. Under General Application Actions, you should click on any action to change it.

Screen off memo

You can write a memo while the screen is off. You need to enable the screen off memo setting.

1. Pick up the S Pen when the screen is off, and write on the screen.

2. Click an option to customize your note:

- Color: Allows you to change the pen color.

- Pen settings: Click to use the pen tool. Then click again to adjust the line thickness.

- Eraser: Click to use the eraser tool. Click again to delete everything.

3. Tap Save to save the note to the Samsung Notes app.

Tip: If your S Pen is removed from your device, even if the screen remains off, you should press the S Pen button and tap the screen to start the note.

Fixed to always-on display

Annotations can be edited or pinned to always appear on the screen.

1. Click "Pin to always display" in the screen off memo.

2. Click Pin to always-on display.

Air command

Use familiar S Pen features like Samsung Notes, Screen Writing, and Smart Select on any screen.

Settings

1. Tap an ⬤ air command or bring the S Pen close to the screen to display the pointer, then press the S Pen button once.

2. You can click any option:

- 🗒️ Create Note: Allows you to open a new note in the Samsung Notes app.

85

- View all notes: Allows you to open the Samsung Notes app and view a list of all notes you have created.

- Smart Selection: Helps draw a portion of the screen to collect into the Gallery app.

- Writing Screen: Helps you take screenshots and draw or write on them.

- Live Message: Allows you to write or create short animated messages using the S Pen.

- AR Graffiti: Use the power of the AR camera to draw interactive graffiti.

- Translate: Hover the S Pen pointer over a word to translate it into another language and hear the pronunciation.

- PENUP: Color, draw, edit and share your live drawings with the S Pen.

- Add: Add to the list of applications and features on the Air command menu.

- ⚙️ Settings: You can change the look and functionality of Air Command, as well as the apps and features it offers.

NFC and payment

The combination of NFC technology and secure payment methods has revolutionized the way we make transactions.

By utilizing Near Field Communication (NFC), it is possible to establish communication with another device without the need for network connectivity. This particular technology is employed by Android Beam as well as specific payment applications. It is important to note that the receiving device must be compatible with NFC and positioned within a proximity of four centimeters from your own device in order for the transfer to occur.

- To enable this feature, go to Settings, tap on 📶 Connections, then select NFC and contactless payments, and toggle the switch to turn it on.

Conveniently make purchases with a simple tap of your device

Tap and pay

Make convenient payments by simply tapping your device onto a credit card reader that is compatible with NFC payment apps.

1. To enable NFC, go to Settings and tap on Connections. From there, navigate to NFC and contactless payments, and simply toggle the switch to turn on NFC.

2. To view the default payment app, simply tap on Contactless payments.

- In order to utilize a different payment application, simply tap on an app that is currently available and select it.

- In order to utilize a payment application that is accessible, simply tap on the option to pay using the currently open app.

- If you wish to designate a different payment service as the default option, simply tap on "Others" and select your preferred service.

Lock screen and security

The lock screen and security measures provide an essential layer of protection for your device.

To ensure the safety of your device and safeguard your valuable data, it is recommended to establish a screen lock.

Different types of screen locks

There are several screen lock options available, each varying in terms of security level: Swipe, Pattern, PIN, Password, and None.

Note: If you're looking to safeguard your device and the confidential information stored within it, consider utilizing biometric locks. These advanced security measures provide an additional layer of protection by utilizing unique biological characteristics. To learn more about the benefits and features of biometric security, be sure to explore this guide on the topic.

Set a secure screen lock

Ensure that you have implemented a strong and reliable lock screen for enhanced security.

To ensure the security of your device, it is advised that you employ a secure screen lock, such as a Pattern, PIN, or Password. This step is essential in order to activate and utilize biometric locks.

1. To set a secure screen lock on your device, navigate to Settings and select 🔒 Lock screen. From there, choose Screen lock type and opt for either a Pattern, PIN, or Password to ensure the security of your device.

2. To display notifications on the lock screen, simply tap ⬤ the option to enable it. You will have the following choices:

- Ensure that notifications are not displayed in the Notification panel, effectively concealing their content.

- Display notifications within the Notification panel.

- Display the content of notifications when the screen is unlocked.

- Select the specific notifications that you would like to be displayed on the Lock screen.

- Enable the option to showcase notifications on the screen of the Always On Display feature.

3. Exit the menu by tapping on Done.

4. Set up the screen lock preferences as follows:

- Automatically unlock your device when it detects trusted locations or other devices. However, please note that you must have a secure screen lock enabled in order to use this convenient smart lock feature.

- Customize your secure lock settings to ensure maximum security. It is important to note that a secure screen lock is necessary in order to utilize this feature effectively.

- To customize the items and appearance of your Lock screen, simply tap on it and make the desired edits.

- To customize the widgets displayed alongside the clock on the Lock screen, simply tap on them.

- By enabling the touch and hold feature, you can decide whether or not to grant permission for editing items on the Lock screen simply by tapping and holding on them.

- Activate the Always On Display feature to keep the screen constantly visible. For additional details, refer to the section on Always On Display.

Restore factory settings password

You can request a passcode to reset your device to factory settings.

- Click on the ⭘"Security & Privacy" in "Settings" > "Additional Security Settings" > "Set/Change Password" and input your desire password.

Set up SIM card lock

You can set a PIN to lock your SIM card to prevent unauthorized use if someone tries to use your SIM card on another device.

- Tap on the ⭘ Security & privacy in Settings > Additional security settings > Set up SIM lock, and go through the directions.
- Tap Lock SIM card to activate this feature.

- Click Change SIM PIN to create a new PIN.

Show password

You can briefly display characters in the password field as you type.

Tap on the ⬤ Security & Privacy in Settings > Additional security settings > Make passwords visible to activate this feature.

Reset to default

Reset device and network settings. You can also reset your device to factory settings.

Reset all settings

You can reset your device to factory settings, which will reset everything except security, language, and account settings. Personal data is not affected.

1. In Settings, click ⬤ General management > Reset > Reset all settings.

2. Click Reset settings and confirm when prompted.

Reset network settings

You can use Reset network settings to reset Wi-Fi, mobile data, and Bluetooth settings.

1. In Settings, click ⚏ General management > Reset > Reset network settings.

2. Click Reset settings and confirm when prompted.

Reset accessibility settings

You can reset your device's accessibility settings. Accessibility settings and your personal information in downloaded apps are not affected.

1. In Settings, click ⚏ General management > Reset > Reset accessibility settings.

2. Click Reset settings and confirm when prompted.

Reset

You can reset your device to factory settings and delete all data from your device.

This action will permanently delete all data from the device, including Google or other account settings, system and app data and settings, downloaded apps, and your music, photos, videos, and other files.

Google Device Protection is automatically activated when you sign in to your Google Account on your device and set the lock screen.

Note that if you reset your Google Account password, it may take 24 hours for the password reset to sync across all devices registered to the account.

Before resetting your device

1. Make sure the information you want to retain has been transferred to your storage area.

2. Sign in to your Google Account and confirm your username and password.

To reset your device

1. In Settings, click ⚏ General management > Reset > Factory reset.

2. Click Reset and follow the instructions to perform the reset.

3. Follow the instructions to setup, if your device restarts.